TRADITIONAL SONGS

She'll Be Coming Around the Mountain

Edited by Ann Owen
Illustrated by Sandra D'Antonio

Music Consultant: Peter Mercer-Taylor, Ph.D.
Associate Professor of Musicology, University of Minnesota
Minneapolis, Minnesota

Reading Consultant: Susan Kesselring, M.A., Literacy Educator
Rosemount-Apple Valley-Eagan (Minnesota) School District

PICTURE WINDOW BOOKS
MINNEAPOLIS, MINNESOTA

Traditional Songs series editor: Peggy Henrikson
Page production: The Design Lab
Musical arrangement: Elizabeth Temple
The illustrations in this book were rendered in pen with digital coloring.

PICTURE WINDOW BOOKS
5115 Excelsior Boulevard
Suite 232
Minneapolis, MN 55416
1-877-845-8392
www.picturewindowbooks.com

Printed in the United States of America.
1 2 3 4 5 6 08 07 06 05 04 03

Library of Congress Cataloging-in-Publication Data
She'll be coming around the mountain / edited by Ann Owen ; illustrated
by Sandra D'Antonio.
p. cm. — (Traditional songs)
Summary: Provides a history and words to six verses of the folk song,
"She'll be Coming Around the Mountain," as well as simple instructions
for making a musical instrument and adding traditional actions and sounds.
Includes bibliographical references (p.).
ISBN 1-4048-0153-7 (library binding)
1. Folk songs, English—United States—History and criticism—Juvenile
literature. 2. Folk dance music—United States—History and criticism—
Juvenile literature. [1. Folk songs—United States.] I. Owen, Ann, 1953-
II. D'Antonio, Sandra, 1956- ill. III. Series.
ML3551 .S546 2003
782.42164'02.68—dc21
2002155436

What do you see when you sing a song? Does the music come in colors?

What do you do when you sing a song? Does the melody make you dance?

What do you hear when you sing a song? Do the words tell a story?

Let's explore the sights and sounds of one of our favorite songs.

Who's coming around the mountain?

Look for the action
cues in the song.

She'll be coming around the mountain when she comes.
She'll be coming around the mountain when she comes.
She'll be coming around the mountain,
she'll be coming around the mountain,
she'll be coming around the mountain when she comes.

4

She'll be driving six white horses when she comes.
She'll be driving six white horses when she comes.
She'll be driving six white horses,
she'll be driving six white horses,
she'll be driving six white horses when she comes.

6

We'll all go out to meet her when she comes.
We'll all go out to meet her when she comes.
We'll all go out to meet her,
we'll all go out to meet her,
we'll all go out to meet her when she comes.

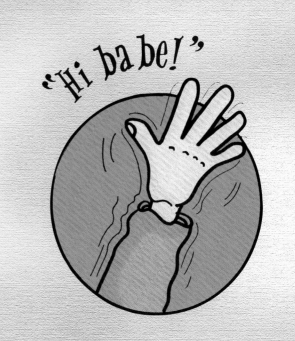

We'll all have chicken and dumplings when she comes.
We'll all have chicken and dumplings when she comes.
We'll all have chicken and dumplings,
we'll all have chicken and dumplings,
we'll all have chicken and dumplings when she comes.

She'll be wearing red pajamas when she comes.
She'll be wearing red pajamas when she comes.
She'll be wearing red pajamas,
she'll be wearing red pajamas,
she'll be wearing red pajamas
when she comes.

"Scratch, scratch"

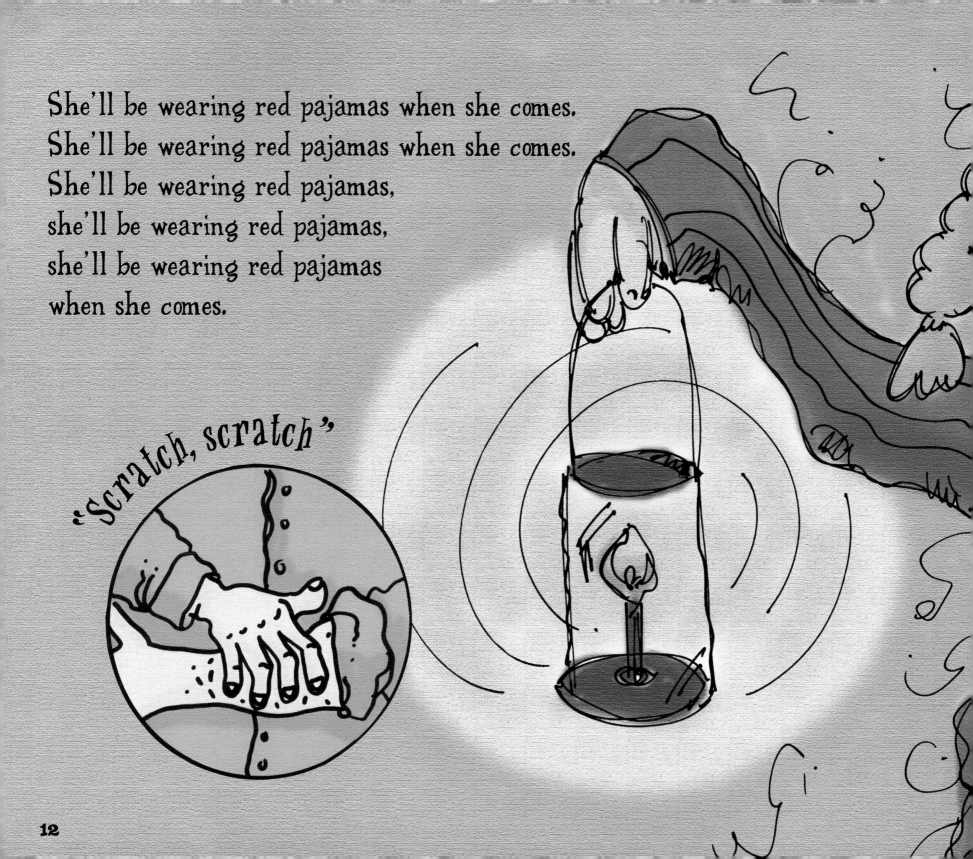

She'll have to sleep with Grandma when she comes.
She'll have to sleep with Grandma when she comes.
She'll have to sleep with Grandma,
she'll have to sleep with Grandma,
she'll have to sleep with Grandma when she comes.

"Snore, snore!"

"Toot, toot!"

16

She'll be coming around the
mountain when she comes.
She'll be coming around the
mountain when she comes.
She'll be coming around the mountain,
she'll be coming around the mountain,
she'll be coming around the
mountain when she comes.

She'll Be Coming Around the Mountain

She'll be co-ming a-round the moun-tain when she comes. She'll be

co-ming a-round the moun-tain when she comes. She'll be

co-ming a-round the moun-tain, she'll be co-ming a-round the moun-tain, she'll be

co-ming a-round the moun-tain when she comes.

2. She'll be driving six white horses when she comes.
She'll be driving six white horses when she comes.
She'll be driving six white horses,
She'll be driving six white horses,
She'll be driving six white horses when she comes.

3. We'll all go out to meet her when she comes.
We'll all go out to meet her when she comes.
We'll all go out to meet her,
We'll all go out to meet her,
We'll all go out to meet her when she comes.

4. We'll all have chicken and dumplings when she comes.
We'll all have chicken and dumplings when she comes.
We'll all have chicken and dumplings,
We'll all have chicken and dumplings,
We'll all have chicken and dumplings when she comes.

5. She'll be wearing red pajamas when she comes.
She'll be wearing red pajamas when she comes.
She'll be wearing red pajamas,
She'll be wearing red pajamas,
She'll be wearing red pajamas when she comes.

6. She'll have to sleep with Grandma when she comes.
She'll have to sleep with Grandma when she comes.
She'll have to sleep with Grandma,
She'll have to sleep with Grandma,
She'll have to sleep with Grandma when she comes.

22

About the Song

"She'll be Coming Around the Mountain" is based on an African-American spiritual, "When the Chariot Comes." It became a popular dance song in the late 1800s. About the same time, it became a favorite with railroad work crews. They added many of the funny verses.

DID YOU KNOW?

It's fun to sing this old song about coming around the mountain, but tunnels made it possible to go right *through* mountains. The world's longest road tunnel is in Laerdal, Norway. It is 15 miles (24 kilometers) long and is built under mountains that rise thousands of feet above the tunnel. When mountain roads are closed because of snow, this tunnel is especially useful. Many towns tucked into valleys among the mountains were very hard to reach before the tunnel was built.

Make a Musical Instrument: Tambourine

WHAT YOU NEED:

- 2 plastic plates or foil pie tins
- paint
- colored construction paper or stickers
- stapler
- dried beans (about two spoonfuls)
- 8 streamers of bright-colored ribbon about 6 inches (15 centimeters) long
- tape or glue

WHAT TO DO:

1. Decorate the bottoms of the plates with colored paper, stickers, or paint. Allow the paint to dry.
2. Put the plates together so that the decorated sides face out. Have an adult help you staple or glue the edges together. Leave an opening at the top.
3. Slide the beans in the opening between the plates. Then finish stapling or gluing the plates shut.
4. Glue or tape the ribbon streamers to the edge of the plates so that they hang down.
5. You're ready to shake and beat your tambourine!

To Learn More

AT THE LIBRARY

Cohn, Amy L. *From Sea to Shining Sea: A Treasury of American Folklore and Folk Songs.* New York: Scholastic, 1993.

Krull, Kathleen. *Gonna Sing My Head Off!: American Folk Songs for Children.* New York: Alfred A. Knopf, 1992.

Lewis, Kevin. *Chugga-Chugga Choo-Choo.* New York: Hyperion Books for Children, 1999.

Mills, Claudia. *Gus and Grandpa Ride the Train.* New York: Farrar, Straus and Giroux, 1998.

Yolen, Jane. *Jane Yolen's Old MacDonald Songbook.* Honesdale, Pa.: Boyds Mills Press, 1994.

ON THE WEB

CHILDREN'S MUSIC WEB
http://www.childrensmusic.org
For resources and links on children's music for kids, parents, educators, and musicians

NATIONAL INSTITUTE OF ENVIRONMENTAL HEALTH SCIENCES KIDS' PAGES: CHILDREN'S SING-ALONG SONGS
http://www.niehs.nih.gov/kids/musicchild.htm
For music and lyrics to many favorite, traditional children's songs

FACT HOUND
Want more information about traditional songs? FACT HOUND offers a safe, fun way to find Web sites. All of the sites on Fact Hound have been researched by our staff. Simply follow these steps:

1. Visit *http://www.facthound.com.*
2. Enter a search word or 1404801537.
3. Click Fetch It.

Your trusty Fact Hound will fetch the best sites for you!